Cello Time Jog

T0083050

Cello accompaniment book

Kathy and David Blackwell

Teacher's note
These duet parts are written to accompany the tunes in *Cello Time Joggers*. They are an alternative to the piano accompaniments or audio tracks, and are not designed to be used with those items.

We are grateful to Alison Ingram and Claire Saddler for all their help in road-testing these duets.

Kathy and David Blackwell

OXFORD
UNIVERSITY PRESS

OXFORD
UNIVERSITY PRESS

Great Clarendon Street, Oxford OX2 6DP,
United Kingdom

Oxford University Press is a department of the University of Oxford.
It furthers the University's objective of excellence in research, scholarship,
and education by publishing worldwide. Oxford is a registered trade mark of
Oxford University Press in the UK and in certain other countries

This collection © Oxford University Press 2002, 2014, and 2022

Unless marked otherwise, all pieces are by Kathy and David Blackwell and are
© Oxford University Press. All traditional and composed pieces are
arranged by Kathy and David Blackwell and are © Oxford University Press.
Unauthorized arrangement or photocopying of this copyright material is ILLEGAL.

Kathy and David Blackwell have asserted their right under the Copyright,
Designs and Patents Act, 1988, to be identified as the Composers of this Work.

Database right Oxford University Press (maker)

Impression: 1

All rights reserved. No part of this publication may be reproduced,
stored in a retrieval system, or transmitted, in any form or by any means,
without the prior permission in writing of Oxford University Press

Permission to perform the works in this anthology in public
(except in the course of divine worship) should normally be obtained from
a local performing right licensing organization, unless the owner or the occupier
of the premises being used already holds a licence from such an organization.
Likewise, permission to make and exploit a recording of these works
should be obtained from a local mechanical copyright licensing organization

Enquiries concerning reproduction outside the scope of the above
should be directed to the Music Rights Department, Oxford University Press, at
music.permissions.uk@oup.com or at the address above

ISBN 978-0-19-356331-5

Cover illustration by Martin Remphry

Music and text origination by Katie Johnston
Printed in Great Britain on acid-free paper by
Halstan & Co. Ltd, Amersham, Bucks.

Contents

1. Bow down, O Belinda 4
2. Under arrest! 4
3. Someone plucks, someone bows 5
4. Down up 5
5. Hill an' gully rider 6
6. Fast lane 6
7. In flight 7
8. Lift off! 8
9. Katie's waltz 8
10. Copy cat 9
11. Rhythm fever 10
12. Here it comes! 11
13. Tap dancer 12
14. So there! 13
15. Rowing boat 14
16. Ally bally 14
17. C string boogie 15
18. Travellin' slow 16
19. Tiptoe, boo! 16
20. Lazy cowboy 18
21. Off to Paris 19
22. City lights 19
23. Clare's song 20
24. Phoebe in her petticoat 21
25. Peace garden 22
26. Summer sun 23
27. On the prowl 24
28. Knock, knock! 24
29. Ready, steady, go now! 25
30. Happy go lucky 26
31. Algy met a bear 27
32. Listen to the rhythm 28
33. Cattle ranch blues 29
34. In the groove 30
35. Stamping dance 31
36. Walking bass 32
37. Chopsticks for two 33
38. Runaway train 34
39. Distant bells 35
40. Lazy scale 36
41. The old castle 37
42. Rocking horse 38
43. Patrick's reel 39
44. Calypso time 40
45. Cello Time 41

Scaley Things 42

1. Bow down, O Belinda

American folk tune

2. Under arrest!

KB & DB

Say the word '*rest*' quietly to yourself as you play.

3. Someone plucks, someone bows

Traditional
Words KB & DB

4. Down up

KB & DB

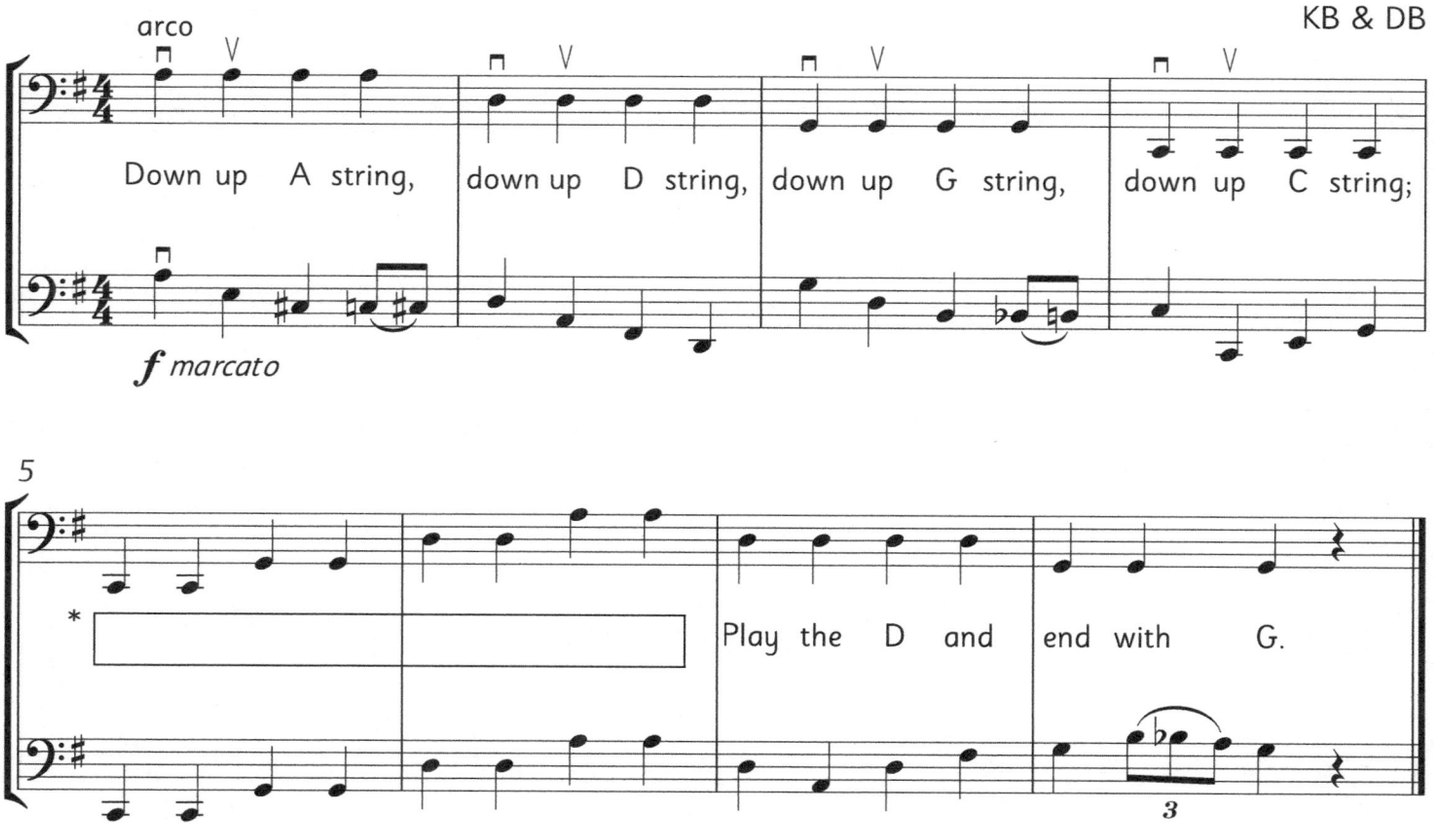

* Fill in the letter names of these notes.

5. Hill an' gully rider

Trad. Jamaican

6. Fast lane

KB & DB

Try even faster the second time through!

7. In flight

Calmly

KB & DB

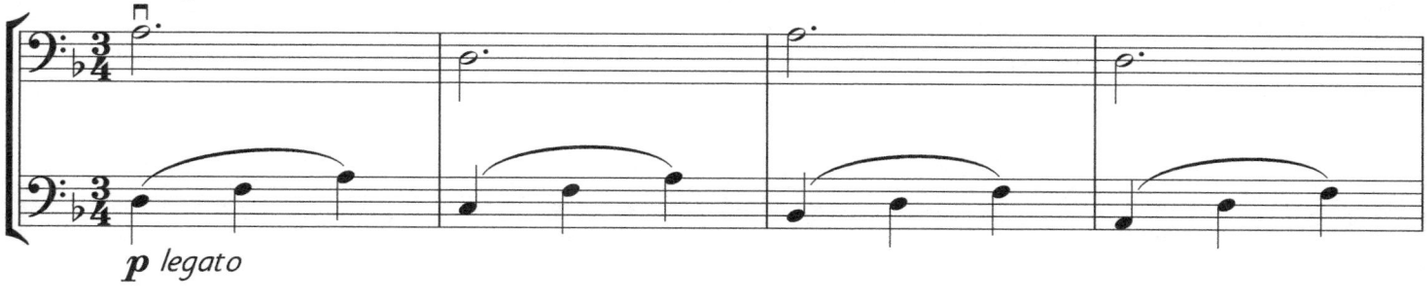

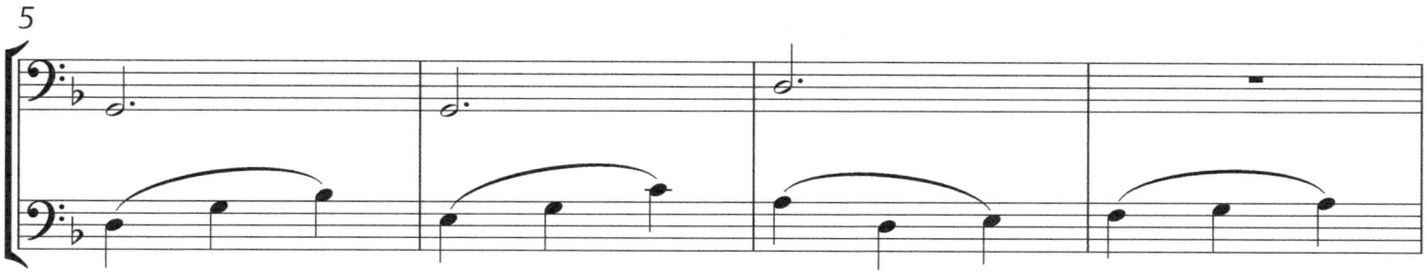

In the rests, let your bow make a circle as you swoop and soar like a bird.

8. Lift off!

Lift your bow off in each of the rests and let it orbit! (Make a circle with your right arm.)

9. Katie's waltz

10. Copy cat

KB & DB

mf

1

G G A A

Can you play what I play? G G A A

5

Fine

Play it now with me.

Can you play what I play?

9

1

D D E E

Can you play what I play? D D E E

13

D.C. al Fine

Play it now with me.

Can you play what I play?

11. Rhythm fever

KB & DB

12. Here it comes!

KB & DB

* Think of a foody rhythm and play it on these notes.

13. Tap dancer

KB & DB

* Tap the cello with your left-hand fingers.

14. So there!

KB & DB

15. Rowing boat

KB & DB

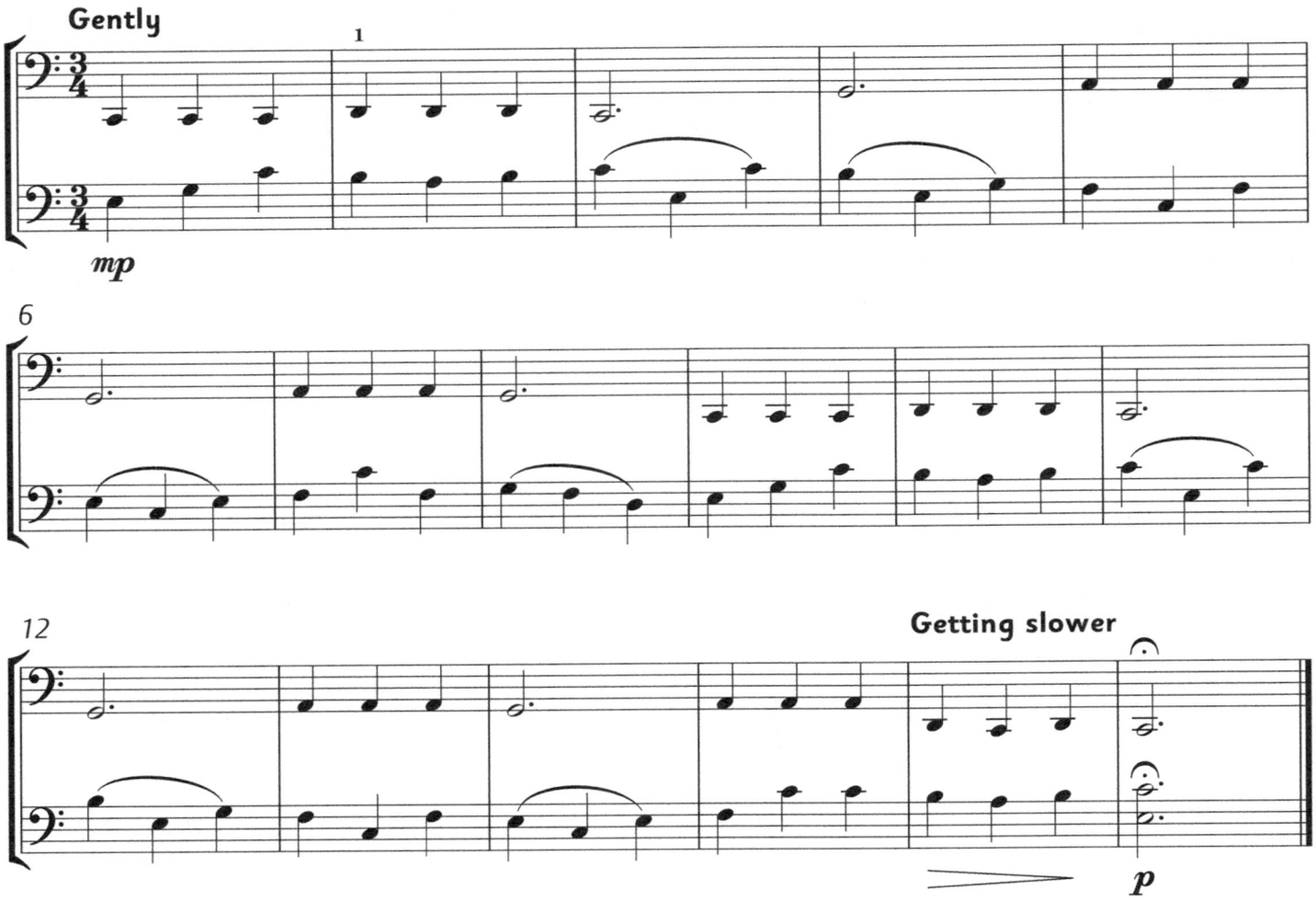

16. Ally bally

Scottish folk tune

17. C string boogie

* Be careful!

18. Travellin' slow

KB & DB

19. Tiptoe, boo!

KB & DB

The pupil's part may also be played pizzicato.

20. Lazy cowboy

21. Off to Paris

French folk tune

22. City lights

KB & DB

23. Clare's song

KB & DB

24. Phoebe in her petticoat

American folk tune

Swap parts when you do the repeat.

25. Peace garden

KB & DB

26. Summer sun

KB & DB

27. On the prowl

KB & DB

28. Knock, knock!

KB & DB

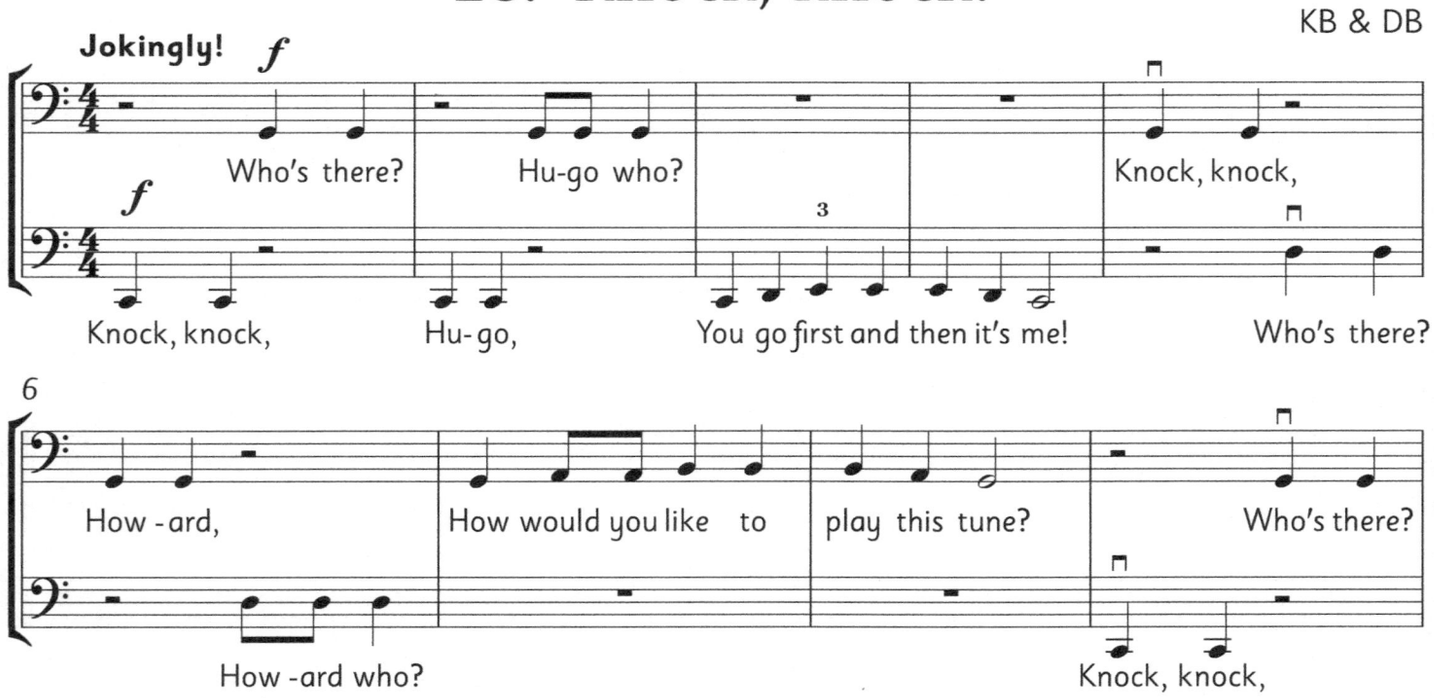

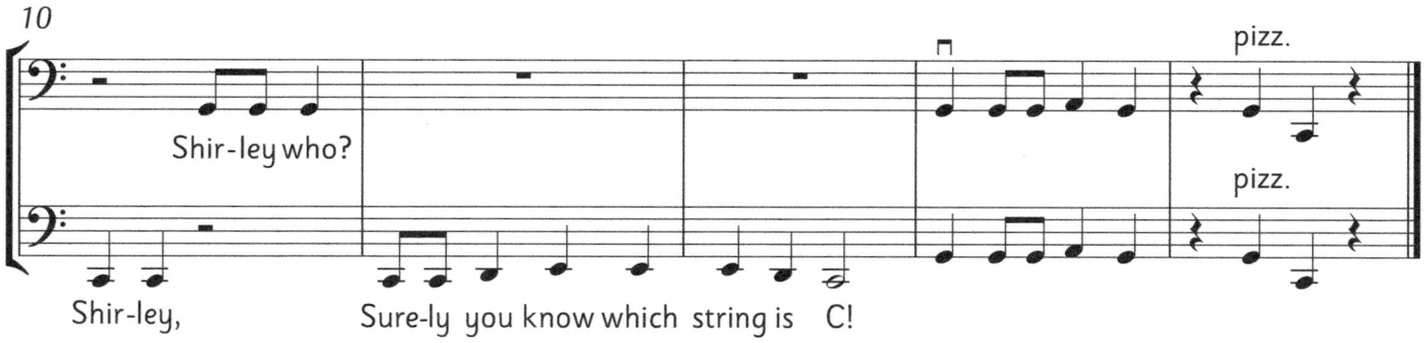

29. Ready, steady, go now!

KB & DB

30. Happy go lucky (for Iain)

KB & DB

31. Algy met a bear

KB & DB
Words anon.

Swap parts when you do the repeat.

32. Listen to the rhythm

KB & DB

33. Cattle ranch blues

KB & DB

34. In the groove

KB & DB

35. Stamping dance

Czech folk tune

36. Walking bass

37. Chopsticks for two

KB & DB

38. Runaway train

KB & DB

39. Distant bells

KB & DB

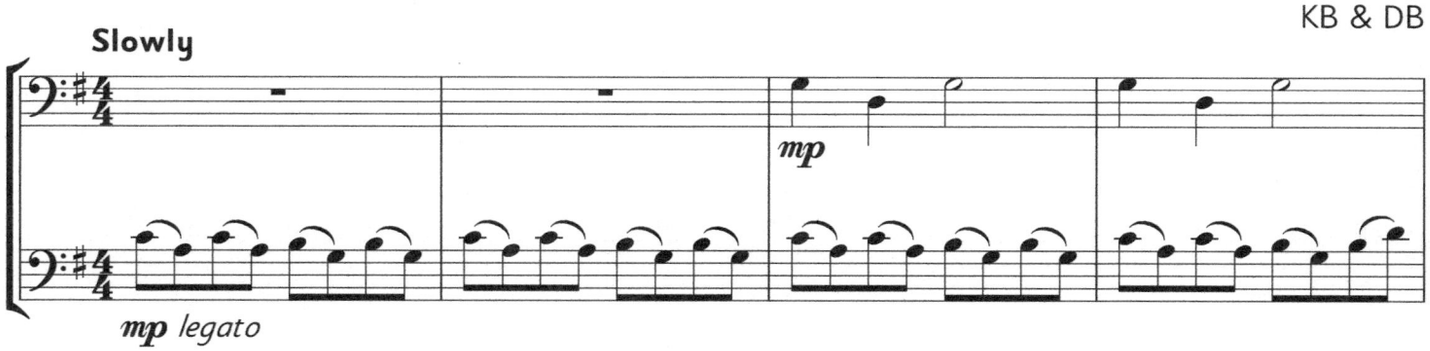

40. Lazy scale

KB & DB

41. The old castle

42. Rocking horse

KB & DB

43. Patrick's reel

44. Calypso time

KB & DB

45. Cello Time

KB & DB

Scaley Things

Super sprinter

KB & DB

Energetically

Wave machine

KB & DB

Ring my number

KB & DB

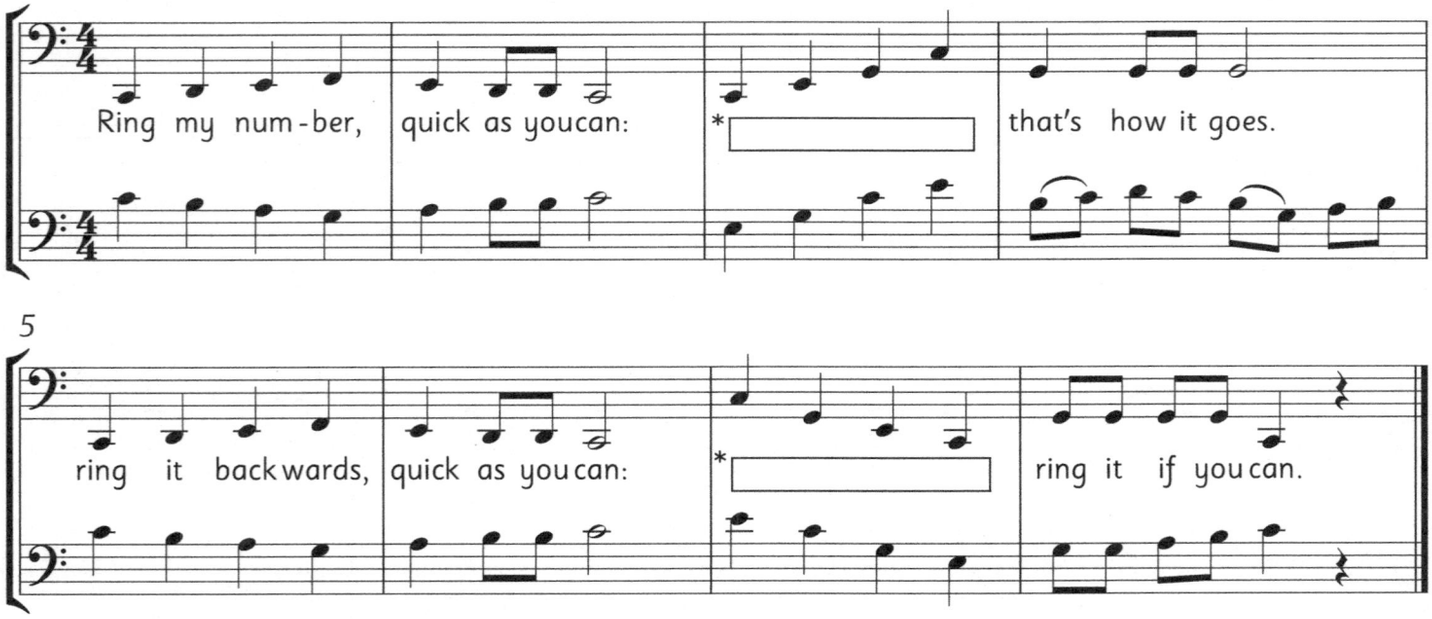

* Use the empty boxes to write in the fingers needed to play these notes.